Tapping RESURRECTION POWER

What really happened in the Garden of Gethsemane

Charles A. West

Pivot Point™
PUBLISHING

PivotPointPublishing.com

Unless otherwise indicated, all scriptural quotations are from the *King James Version* of the Bible.

Scripture verses marked TLB are taken from the Living Bible. The Living Bible copyright © 1971 by Tyndale House Foundation. Used by permission of Tyndale House Publishers Inc., Carol Stream, Illinois 60188. All rights reserved.

Old Testament Scripture verses marked AMP are taken from the Amplified Bible, Old Testament, copyright © 1965, 1987 by Zondervan Corporation. New Testament Scripture verses marked AMP are taken from the Amplified Bible, New Testament, copyright © 1954, 1958, 1987 by Lockman Foundation. Used by permission of Zondervan Publishing House.

Tapping Resurrection Power
What Really Happened in the Garden of Gethsemane
Published by:
Pivot Point Publishing
Sapulpa, OK 74066
PivotPointPublishing.com
ISBN 978-0-692-32649-7

Book production by:
Silver Lining Creative
A Division of Pivot Point Publishing
www.silverliningcreative.com

Printed in the United States of America.

Prelude

When we enter the Garden of Gethsemane, we will see many things that have been hidden in the scriptures as the Holy Spirit unveils them for us. The Holy Spirit will also shine a light on many other hidden truths throughout this book.

Scriptures paint pictures in our hearts. This is a book of scriptures that have been placed in a proper sequence, to paint picture after picture, to make it easier for us to see their true meaning, as the Holy Spirit unveils them for us.

Table of Contents

Preface

It is evident we are living in a time when the Holy Spirit is illuminating all the scriptures that have been hidden for the end time generation; scriptures concerning end time events, and scriptures that will be used for the end time harvest.

This message shines a bright light on Jesus Christ as the Messiah, the Lord and Savior to all the people who choose Him. I believe this message will be used like a giant combine to help bring in the end time harvest.

— *Charles A. (Chuck) West*

Introduction

When I received the New Birth, and the Holy Bible started to be my guide and the Holy Spirit my teacher, I was thrilled and still am.

I also found out there were great books and study guides, and teachers that the Holy Spirit used to help us understand the hidden truths in God's Word.

I never dreamed that I would write a book, but when the Holy Spirit would show me things that were hidden in His Word, hidden truths that I had never seen written in a book or heard from the pulpit, I wanted to share them.

I had a few friends I could share them with, but after that list ran out it was over. I wasn't satisfied; in my heart I knew the Father wanted these truths shared.

All of a sudden my greatest desire was to write a book and make these hidden truths available to everyone. We need to remember these truths weren't hidden from God's kids, they were hidden for us.

This is my second book, Glory to God the Father.

— *Chuck West*

Chapter 1
The Abrahamic Covenant

The Lord speaking to Abraham:

"And I will establish my covenant between me and thee and thy seed after thee in their generations for an everlasting covenant, to be a God unto thee, and to thy seed after thee."

Genesis 17:7

"And God said unto Abraham, "Thou shalt keep my covenant therefore, thou, and thy seed after thee in their generations."

"This is my covenant, which ye shall keep, between me and you and thy seed after thee; Every man child among you shall be circumcised."

"And ye shall circumcise the flesh of your foreskin; and it shall be a token of the covenant betwixt me and you."

Genesis 17:9-11

"And God said, Sarah thy wife shall bear thee a son indeed; and thou shalt call his name Isaac: and I will establish my covenant with him for an everlasting covenant, and with his seed after him."

Genesis 17:19

"And the Lord said, Shall I hide from Abraham that thing which I do; Seeing that Abraham shall

1

surely become a great and mighty nation, and all the nations of the earth shall be blessed in him?"

"For I know him, that he will command his children and his household after him, and they shall keep the way of the Lord, to do justice and judgment; that the Lord may bring upon Abraham that which he hath spoken of him."

Genesis 18:17-19

This is the reason God chose Abraham and his seed out of all the men on the earth to make a covenant with. God already knew Abraham and his seed would keep the covenant.

"And it came to pass after these things, that God did tempt [test] Abraham, and said unto him, Abraham: and he said, Behold, here I am."

"And he said, Take now thy son, thine only son Isaac, whom thou lovest, and get into the land of Moriah; and offer him there for a burnt offering upon one of the mountains which I will tell thee of."

"And Abraham rose up early in the morning, and saddled his ass, and took two of his young men with him, and Isaac his son, and clave [split] the wood for the burnt offering, and rose up, and went unto the place of which God had told him."

"Then on the third day Abraham lifted up his eyes, and saw the place afar off."

"And Abraham said unto his young men, Abide ye here with the ass; and I and the lad will go yonder and worship, and come again to you."

"And Abraham took the wood of the burnt offering, and laid it upon Isaac his son; and he took the fire in his hand, and a knife; and they went both of them together."

"And Isaac spake unto Abraham his father, and said, My father: and he said, Here am I, my son. And he said, behold the fire and the wood: but where is the lamb for a burnt offering?"

"And Abraham said, My son, God will provide himself a lamb for a burnt offering: so they went both of them together."

"And they came to the place which God had told him of; and Abraham built an altar there, and laid the wood in order, and bound Isaac his son, and laid him on the altar upon the wood." [Isaac was obedient to his father, even unto death.]

"And Abraham stretched forth his hand and took the knife to slay his son."

"And the angel of the Lord called unto him out of heaven and said, Abraham, Abraham: and he said, Here am I."

"And he said, Lay not thine hand upon the lad, neither do thou anything unto him: for now I know that thou fearest God, seeing thou hast not withheld thy son, thine only son from me."

"And Abraham lifted up his eyes, and looked, and behold behind him a ram caught in a thicket by his horns: and Abraham went and took the ram, and offered him up for a burnt offering in the stead of his son."

"And Abraham called the name of the place Jehovah-Jireh: [The Lord will provide] as it is said unto this day, In the mount of the Lord it shall be seen."

"And the angel of the Lord called unto Abraham out of heaven the second time,"

Genesis 22:1-15

"And said, <u>By</u> <u>myself</u> have I sworn, saith the Lord, for because thou hast done this thing, and hast not withheld thy son, thine only son:"

"That in blessing I will bless thee, and in multiplying I will multiply thy seed as the stars of the heaven, and as the sand which is upon the sea shore; and thy seed shall possess the gate of his enemies:"

"And in thy seed shall <u>all</u> <u>the</u> <u>nations</u> of the earth be blessed; because thou hast obeyed my voice."

Genesis 22:16-18

"And he said unto Abram, know of a surety that thy seed shall be a stranger in a land that is not theirs, and shall serve them; and they shall afflict them four hundred years;" [captivity in Egypt]

"And also that nation, whom they shall serve, will I judge: and afterward shall they come out with great substance."

Genesis 15:13,14

"And it came to pass in process of time, that the King of Egypt died: and the children of Israel sighed by reason of the bondage, and they cried, and their cry came up unto God by reason of the bondage."

"And God heard their groaning, and <u>God</u> <u>remembered</u> <u>his</u> <u>covenant</u> with Abraham, with Isaac, and with Jacob."

Exodus 2:23,24

"And the Lord said, I have surely <u>seen</u> the affliction of <u>my</u> <u>people</u> which are in Egypt, and have <u>heard</u> their cry by reason of their taskmasters; for I know their sorrows;"

"And I am come down to deliver them out of the hand of the Egyptians, and to bring them up out of that land unto a good land and a large, unto a land flowing with milk and honey;"

Exodus 3:7,8

Remember, our God is a **covenant keeping God.**

Chapter 2
The Mosaic Law Concerning the Sin Offerings

Concerning the Priesthood, the Lord speaks to Moses:

"And thou shalt bring Aaron and his sons unto the door of the tabernacle of the congregation, and wash them with water."

"And thou shalt put upon Aaron the holy garments, and anoint him, and sanctify him; that he may minister unto me in the priest's office."

"And thou shalt bring his sons, and clothe them with coats;"

"And thou shalt anoint them, as thou didst anoint their father, that they may minister unto me in the priest's office: for their anointing shall surely be an everlasting priesthood throughout their generations."

Exodus 40:12-15

In Leviticus chapter 8, the Lord speaks to Moses and tells him to consecrate Aaron and his sons, and to pour the anointing oil upon Aaron's head.

"And he [Moses] poured of the anointing oil upon Aaron's head, and anointed him to sanctify him."

Leviticus 8:12

"And he that is the high priest among his brethren, upon whose head the anointing oil was poured, and that is consecrated to put on the garments, shall not uncover his head, nor rend his clothes;"

Leviticus 21:10

Atonement in the Holy Place

"Thus shall Aaron come into the holy place: with a young bullock for a sin offering, and a ram for a burnt offering."

"He shall put on the holy linen coat, and he shall have the linen breeches upon his flesh, and shall be girded with a linen girdle, and with the linen mitre shall he be attired: these are holy garments; therefore shall he wash his flesh in water, and so put them on."

"And he shall take of the congregation of the children of Israel two kids of the goats for a sin offering, and one ram for a burnt offering."

"And Aaron shall offer his bullock of the sin offering, which is for himself, and make an atonement for himself, and for his house."

"And he shall take the two goats, and present them before the Lord at the door of the tabernacle of the congregation."

"And Aaron shall cast lots upon the two goats; one lot for the Lord, and the other lot for the scape goat."

"And Aaron shall bring the goat upon which the Lord's lot fell, and offer him for a sin offering."

"But the goat, on which the lot fell to be the scapegoat, shall be presented alive before the Lord, to make an atonement with him, and to let him go for a scapegoat into the wilderness."

Leviticus 16:3-10

Once a year, this sacrifice was for God's covenant people. The blood of the scapegoat (the sin bearer) was never used in the holy place or within the veil before the mercy seat.

The sin offerings in Leviticus had a very important thing in common. The **blood** from the animal that became sin or that carried the sins out of the camp, wasn't allowed in the tabernacle or the Holy of Holies. (Remember this.)

Another scripture that bears this out is Leviticus 4:29,30.

> **"And he** [the priest] **shall lay his hand upon the head of the sin offering, and slay the sin offering in the place of the burnt offering."**

> **"And the priest shall take of the blood thereof with his finger, and put it upon the horns of the altar of burnt offering, and shall pour out all the blood thereof at the bottom of the altar."**

The blood that carried the sins was never allowed to be brought into the holy place. (Remember this.) Other scriptures you can check are Leviticus 4:7,18 and 34.

> **"Then came the soldiers, and brake the legs of the first, and of the other which was crucified with him."**

> **"But when they came to Jesus, they saw that he was dead already, they brake not his legs:"**

> **"But one of the soldiers with a spear, pierced his side, and forthwith came there out blood and water."**
>
> **John 19:32-34**

The cross where Jesus was crucified was the altar upon which he was sacrificed. When the blood flowed out of his side, it flowed to the bottom of the cross (altar.) This blood was carrying the sins of the world at this time. (Remember this for later.)

7

Leviticus 17:11 "For the life of the flesh is in the blood: and I have given it to you upon the altar to make an atonement for your souls: for it is the blood that maketh an atonement for the soul."

Chapter 3
The Promises

"Even as Abraham BELIEVED God, AND IT WAS ACCOUNTED TO HIM FOR RIGHTEOUSNESS."

"Know ye therefore that they which are of faith, [born again] the same are the children of Abraham."

"And the scripture, foreseeing that God would justify the heathen through faith, preached before the gospel unto Abraham, saying, In thee shall all nations be blessed."

"So then, they which be of <u>faith</u> [born again] are blessed with faithful Abraham." [become Abraham's seed]

"For as many as are of the works of the Law are under the curse: for it is written, CURSED IS EVERY ONE THAT CONTINUETH NOT IN ALL THINGS WHICH ARE WRITTEN IN THE BOOK OF THE LAW TO DO THEM."

"But that no man is justified by the law in the sight of God, it is evident: for, The <u>just</u> shall live by faith." [faith that Jesus is Lord]

"And the Law is not of faith: but, THE MAN THAT DOETH THEM SHALL LIVE IN THEM."

"Christ hath redeemed us from the curse of the Law, being made a curse for us: for it is written, CURSED IS EVERY ONE THAT HANGETH ON A TREE:" [is crucified]

"That the blessings of Abraham might come on the Gentiles through Jesus Christ; that we might receive the promise of the Spirit through faith." [the new birth]

"Brethren, I speak after the manner of men; Though it be but a man's covenant, yet if it be confirmed, no man disannulleth, or addeth thereto."

"Now to Abraham and his <u>seed</u> were the promises made. He saith not, and to seeds, as of many: but as of one, And to thy seed, which is Christ." [Jesus Christ is the seed of Abraham.]

Galatians 3:6-16

"And if ye be Christ's, then are ye Abraham's seed, and heirs according to the promise." [of the new birth]

Galatians 3:29

Chapter 4
The Incarnation

"In the beginning was the Word, and the Word was with God, and the <u>Word</u> <u>was</u> <u>God</u>."

"The same was in the beginning with God."

John 1:1,2

"And the Word was made flesh, and dwelt among us, (and we beheld his glory, the glory as of the only begotten of the Father,) full of grace and truth."

John 1:14

"Wherefore when he [the Word] cometh into the world, he saith, SACRIFICE AND OFFERING THOU WOULDEST NOT, BUT A BODY HAST THOU PREPARED ME:"

"IN BURNT OFFERINGS AND SACRIFICES FOR SIN THOU HAST HAD NO PLEASURE."

"THEN SAID I, LO, I COME (IN THE VOLUME OF THE BOOK IT IS WRITTEN OF ME) TO DO THY WILL, O GOD."

"Above when he said, Sacrifice and offering and burnt offerings and offering for sin thou wouldest not, neither hadst pleasure therein; which are offered by the law;"

"Then said he, Lo, I come to do thy will, O God. He taketh away the first, [covenant] that he may establish the second." [covenant]

"By the which will we are sanctified through the offering of the body of Jesus Christ once for all."

Hebrews 10:5-10

11

"That at that time ye were without Christ, being aliens from the commonwealth of Israel, and strangers from the covenants of promise, having no hope, and without God in the world:"

"But now in Christ Jesus ye who sometimes were far off [without a covenant] are made nigh by the blood [life] of Christ."

"For he is our peace, who hath made both one, and hath broken down the middle wall of partition between us:"

"Having abolished in his flesh the enmity, even the law of commandments contained in ordinances; for to make [create] in himself of twain [two] one new man, so making peace;" [this is the incarnation]

"And that he might reconcile both [Jews and Gentiles] unto God in one body by the cross, having slain the enmity [reason for opposition] thereby:"

Ephesians 2:12-16

God had prepared a body for Jesus through Abraham's seed. The Word laid down his glory and entered this body. The two (twain) became one. Jesus was a new creation, a perfect man. Jesus Christ not only had a perfect body, he also had God's nature and God's spirit. Jesus was Abraham's seed; a product of Abraham and God, full of God's life, spirit, and nature.

"And so it is written, The first man, Adam, was made a living soul; the last Adam [Jesus Christ] was made a quickening [life giving] spirit."

1 Corinthians 15:45

17 "For if by one man's offence [Adam]death reigned by one; much more they which receive abundance of grace and of the gift of righteousness shall reign in life by one Jesus Christ.)

18 "Therefore as by the offense of one [Adam] judgment came upon all men to condemnation; even so by the righteousness of one [Jesus] the free gift came upon all men unto justification of life."

19 "For as by one man's disobedience many were made sinners, so by the <u>obedience</u> of one shall many be made righteous."

Romans 5:17-19

Chapter 5
Power to Take It Up Again

"Therefore doth my Father love me, [Jesus] because I lay down my life, that I might take it again."

"No man taketh it from me, but I lay it down of myself. I have power to lay it down, and I have power to take it again. This <u>commandment</u> have I received of my Father."

John 10:17,18

Strong's Concordance Greek Dictionary of the New Testament says the word commandment (1785) used in verse eighteen is "an authoritative prescription:" What was this authoritative prescription? What gave Jesus the power to be instrumental in taking his life again?

Let's keep reading and the Holy Spirit will illuminate these scriptures for us.

Chapter 6
Building Faith and Confidence

"And David said unto Saul, Thy servant kept his father's sheep, and there came a lion, and a bear, and took a lamb out of the flock:"

"And I went out after him, and smote him, and delivered it out of his mouth: and when he arose against me, I caught him by his beard, and smote him, and slew him."

"Thy servant slew both the lion and the bear: and this uncircumcised Philistine shall be as one of them, seeing he has defied the armies of the living God."

David said, "Moreover, the Lord that delivered me out of the paw of the lion, and out of the paw of the bear, he will deliver me out of the hand of this Philistine. And Saul said unto David, go and the Lord be with thee."

1 Samuel 17:34-37

When the Lord delivered David out of the paw of the lion, and out of the paw of the bear, it gave David the faith and confidence that the Lord would deliver him out of the hand of Goliath. It's evident David had been prepared for this very moment.

The term uncircumcised Philistine is referring to a man that doesn't have a covenant with God.

"When he [Jesus] had heard therefore that he [Lazarus] was sick, he abode two days still in the same place where he was."
                                                                                                    John 11:6

What did Jesus do those two days? He interceded in the spirit to loose the power of God to raise Lazarus from the dead, and he was heard.

"Then when Jesus came, he found that he had lain in the grave four days already."
                                                                                                    John 11:17

"When Jesus therefore saw her weeping, [Mary, sister of Lazarus] **and the Jews also weeping which came with her, he groaned in the Spirit and was troubled.**

"And said, Where have ye laid him? They said unto him, Lord come and see."

"Jesus wept." [<u>still</u> <u>interceding</u>]

"Then said the Jews, behold how he loved him!"

And some of them said, Could not this man, which opened the eyes of the blind, have caused that even this man should not have died?"

"Jesus therefore again <u>groaning</u> in himself cometh to the grave. It was a cave, and a stone lay upon it."

"Jesus said, take ye away the stone. Martha, the sister of him that was dead, saith unto him, Lord, by this time he stinketh: for he as been dead four days."
                                                                                                    John 11:33-39

I looked up the word groaning used in the above scriptures in Strong's Concordance (4726 in the Greek Dictionary.) Its definition was "a sigh." It also said 4726 came from 4727. Its definition is "pray inaudibly."

"Likewise the Spirit also helpeth our infirmities: for we know not what we should pray for as we ought: but the Spirit itself maketh intercession for us with groanings which <u>cannot</u> <u>be</u> <u>uttered</u>.
                                                                                                    Romans 8:26

The word utterance means to enunciate plainly. Enunciate means to pronounce words clearly and distinctly. When we groan in the Spirit and pray in other tongues, we bypass our brain and let the Holy Spirit give the utterance (the meaning) to the sounds that we make, which is the perfect will of God. This kind of praying takes your most holy faith.

"But ye, beloved, building up yourselves on your most holy faith, praying in the Holy Ghost."
Jude 1:20

And he that searcheth the hearts knoweth what is the mind of the Spirit, because he maketh intercession for the saints according to the will of God."
Romans 8:27

"Then they took away the stone from the place where the dead was laid. And Jesus lifted up his eyes, and said, Father, I thank thee that thou hast heard me."

"And I knew that thou hearest me always: but because of the people which stand by I said it, that they may believe that thou hast sent me."

"And when he thus had spoken, he cried with a loud voice, Lazarus, come forth."

"And he that was dead came forth, bound hand and foot with graveclothes: and his face was bound about with a napkin. Jesus saith unto them, loose him, and let him go."
John 11:41-44

Jesus had loosed the power of God to raise Lazarus from the dead, by praying with all prayer and supplication in the Spirit. This was just a few days before Jesus was to die on the cross. We need to remember Jesus was operating with the power of a man walking the earth filled with the Holy Spirit; the same power that a man has today when he's born again and filled with the Holy Spirit. Yes, Jesus was being prepared for the battle that was to take place in a few days at Gethsemane.

Chapter 7
Jesus Prays Before Entering the Garden of Gethsemane

We should read this prayer.

"These words spake Jesus, and lifted up his eyes to heaven, and said, Father, the hour is come; glorify thy Son, that thy Son also may glorify thee:"

"As thou hast given him power over all flesh, that he should give eternal life to as many as thou hast given him."

"And this is life eternal, that they might know thee the only true God, and Jesus Christ, whom thou hast sent."

"I have glorified thee on the earth: I have finished the work which thou gavest me to do."

"And now, O Father, glorify thou me with thine own self <u>with the glory which I had with thee before the world was.</u>"

"I have manifested thy name unto the men which thou gavest me out of the world: thine they were, and thou gavest them me; and they have kept thy word."

"Now they have known that all things whatsoever thou hast given me are of thee."

"For I have given unto them the words which thou gavest me; and they have received them, and have known surely <u>that</u> I <u>came</u> <u>out</u> <u>from</u> <u>thee</u>, and they have believed that thou didst send me."

"I pray for them: I pray not for the world, but for them which thou hast given me; for they are thine."

"And all mine are thine, and thine are mine; and I am glorified in them."

"And now I am no more in the world, but these are in the world, and I come to thee. Holy Father, keep through thine own name those whom thou hast given me, that they may be one, as we are."

"While I was with them in the world, I kept them in thy name: those that thou gavest me I have kept, and none of them is lost, but the son of perdition; that the scripture might be fulfilled."

"And now come I to thee; and these things I speak in the world, that they might have my joy fulfilled in themselves."

"I have given them thy word; and the world hath hated them, because they are not of the world, even as I am not of the world."

"I pray not that they shouldest take them out of the world, but that thou shouldest keep them from the evil." [<u>one</u>]

"They are not of the world, even as I am not of the world."

"Sanctify them through thy truth: thy word is truth."

"As thou hast sent me into the world, even so have I also sent them into the world."

"And for their sakes I sanctify myself, that they also might be sanctified through the truth."

"<u>Neither</u> <u>pray</u> I <u>for</u> <u>these</u> <u>alone</u>, but for them also which shall believe on me through their word;"

That they all may be one; as thou, Father art in me, and I in thee, that they also may be one in us: that the world may believe that thou hast sent me."

"And the glory which thou gavest me I have given them: that they may be one, even as we are one:"

I in them, and thou in me, that they may be made perfect in one; and that the world may know that thou hast sent me, and hast loved them, as thou hast loved me.

"Father, I will that they also, whom thou hast given me, be with me where I am; that they may behold my glory, which thou hast given me: for thou lovest me before the foundation of the world."

"O righteous Father, the world hath not known thee: but I have known thee, and these have known that thou hast sent me."

"And I have declared unto them thy name, and will declare it: that the love wherewith thou hast loved me may be in them, and I in them."

John 17:1-26

Jesus goes onto Gethesmane.

Chapter 8
Gethsemane:
Tapping Resurrection Power

A reminder of things we should know and look for as we enter the Garden of Gethsemane.

In Genesis 17:7 God makes a covenant with Abraham.

Then God speaks to Abraham in Genesis 17:19, "And God said, Sarah thy wife shall bear thee a son indeed; and thou shall call his name Isaac: and I will **establish** my covenant with him for an everlasting covenant, **and with his seed** after him."

Why did God choose Abraham for this covenant? In Genesis 18:19 God says, "**For I know him**, that he will command his children and his household after him, and **they shall keep the way** of the Lord, to do justice and judgment; that the Lord may bring upon Abraham that which he hath spoken of him." God knew that Abraham would keep the covenant he had made with him.

God **proves** Abraham will keep the covenant He made with him. In Genesis 22:2-12 God tells Abraham to take his only begotten son Isaac to a mountain in the Land of Moriah and to offer him as a burnt offering. When they came to the mountain, Abraham took the wood he had for the burnt offering and **laid** it upon Isaac his son to carry up the mountain. Abraham was approximately 120 years old and Isaac was a strong young man and able to carry the load. When they reached the right spot, Abraham built an altar there, and laid the wood in order. Isaac had asked his father where the lamb was for the burnt offering. Isaac was a strong young man; he didn't have to let his older father bind him and offer him as a burnt offering to God.

Isaac was obedient to his father, even unto death. God had established his covenant with Isaac, Abraham's only son, as spoken of in Genesis 17:19. Isaac's life wouldn't save mankind, but now God had a legal right to use a body produced by Abraham's seed, when the time was right.

God could create a body for Jesus, but then the covenant wouldn't be valid. The body had to come from Abraham's seed, through Sarah his wife.

Abraham was obedient to offer his only begotten son as a burnt offering to God. Isaac was obedient to give his life to his father. This will shine a light on what happened in the Garden of Gethsemane. This is a type and shadow of what would happen at the Garden of Gethsemane.

Jesus would be obedient to His Father even unto death. God the Father would offer his only begotten to save the world.

This is what must be accomplished at Gethsemane:

In the Garden of Gethsemane, Jesus lays down his life, by consecrating through prayer, his life into his Father's hands, praying, "Not my will but thine be done." Jesus is obedient to suffer and die spiritually and physically on the cross for the sins of all people who will call Him Lord.

In the Garden of Gethsemane, the Father accepts his offer and cuts the covenant with Abraham and Abraham's seed which is Christ. Great drops of blood flowed from Jesus' body as the covenant was cut. Later this blood was carried into heaven to the heavenly Holy of Holies where Jesus would sprinkle it on the mercy seat. This blood represented the life of a perfect man who had never sinned, the Son of God, Jesus Christ, who was also the seed of Abraham. When this blood was sprinkled on the mercy seat, it would complete and seal the Abrahamic Covenant. We could then be heirs to the new covenant as the seed of Abraham.

Now the Father could offer His son as a sacrifice for the sins of the world.

> **"For God so loved the world, that he gave his only begotten Son, that whosoever believeth in him should not perish, but have everlasting life."**

> **"For God sent not his Son into the world to condemn the world; but that the world through him might be saved."**
>
> **John 3:16,17**

Jesus had lain down his life through prayers of consecration. "Not my will, but thine be done." Jesus had said, "I have the power to lay my life down." Jesus also said, "I have the power to take it up again." Jesus had to do this **before** he died spiritually and physically.

After Jesus had laid his life down through prayer at Gethsemane, he had to take it up again through prayer. This is the prayer Jesus prayed at Gethsemane that loosed the Holy Spirit to save him out from death.

> **"In the days of his flesh [Jesus] offered up definite, special petitions [for that which He not only wanted but needed], and supplications, with strong crying and tears, to Him who was [always] able to save Him (out) from death, and He was heard because of His reverence toward God — His godly fear, His piety, [that is, in that He shrank from the horrors of separation from the bright presence of the Father]."**
>
> **Hebrews 5:7 (AMP)**

With this in mind, let's go back to the scriptures and follow Jesus into and through Gethsemane. Jesus was with his desciples, except for Judas.

> **"And they came to a place which was named Gethsemane: and he saith to his disciples, sit ye here, while I shall pray."**

> **"And he taketh with him Peter and James and John, and began to be sore amazed, and to be very heavy;"** [greatly troubled and deeply distressed]
>
>

Mark 14:32,33

Why?

> **"And I say unto you my friends, Be not afraid of <u>them</u> that kill the body, and after that have no more that <u>they</u> can do."**

> **"But I will forewarn you whom ye shall fear: <u>Fear him</u>, which after he hath killed hath power to cast into hell; yea, I say unto you, Fear him."** [Satan]
>
> **Luke 12:4,5**

These scriptures let us know why Jesus was deeply distressed. Evidently it was possible for Jesus, who was operating with the power of a man filled with the Holy Spirit, to **lose** this final battle.

> **"And he [Jesus] was withdrawn from them about a stone's cast, and kneeled down, and prayed,"**

> **"Saying, Father, if thou be willing, remove this cup from me: nevertheless, not my will, but thine be done."** [Jesus is being obedient unto death, laying his life down through prayer.]

> **"And there appeared an angel unto him from heaven, strengthening him."**

> **"And being in an agony he prayed more earnestly: and his sweat was as it were <u>great</u> <u>drops</u> <u>of</u> <u>blood</u> falling down to the ground."** [The Father God was cut-

ting the Abrahamic Covenant with Abraham and Abraham's seed which is Jesus Christ.]

Luke 22:41-44

This was his third hour of prayer. Jesus was praying a prayer of consecration, a dedicatory sacrifice of his life into God's hand. Remember, Jesus said, "I have the **power** to lay my life down, and the **power** to take it up again." This is where Jesus **laid his life down**, by placing it into the Father's hand, through prayer.

When the great drops of blood flowed from Jesus' body, the Father had accepted his life. Remember, the life of the flesh is in the blood. This blood came from a perfect man, a spiritual man, filled with the Spirit of God, a man without sin, a man without sickness or disease. This blood was from Jesus Christ who is Abraham's seed. This blood would seal the New Covenant, when Jesus sprinkled it on the real Mercy Seat in heaven.

"But now in Christ Jesus ye who sometimes were far off are made nigh by the blood of Christ."

"For he is our peace, who hath <u>made</u> <u>both</u> <u>one</u>, [Jews and Gentiles] **and hath broken down the middle wall of partition** [division] **between us."**

"Having abolished in his flesh the enmity, even the law of commandments contained in ordinances; for to make [create] **in himself of <u>twain</u>** [the two] **one new man,** [creation] **so making peace;"**

"And that he might reconcile <u>both</u> [Jews and Gentiles] **unto God in one body by the cross, having slain the enmity thereby:"**

Ephesians 2:13-16

Remember, through Abraham came the body, the **Word** entered the body. The (twain) **two became one**. The one was Christ. Christ was Abraham's seed, and God's seed, the two were made one. Jesus Christ was the best Abraham could give and the best God could give.

> "And if ye be Christ's, then are ye Abraham's seed, and heirs according to the promise."
>
> **Galatians 3:29**

While Jesus was still praying in the Garden of Gethsemane, it was time to take his life up. He did it the same way he laid his life down. He did it through prayer.

> "In the days of his <u>flesh</u> [Jesus] offered up definite, special petitions [for that which He not only wanted but needed], and supplications, with strong crying and tears, to Him who was [always] able to save Him (out) from death, and <u>He</u> <u>was</u> <u>heard</u> because of His reverence toward God — His godly fear, His piety, [that is, in that He shrank from the horrors of separation from the bright presence of the Father]."
>
> **Hebrews 5:7 (AMP)**

This prayer was while Jesus was in Gethsemane. He was still alive in the **flesh**, and he was heard. Jesus had prayed through. He had beaten hell, death and the grave before he was crucified.

Jesus, operating with the power of a man filled with the Holy Spirit, praying with all prayer and supplication in the Spirit, gave the Father God the legal authority to raise him from the dead. **Jesus had tapped resurrection power as a man.** A man had lost dominion, and a man won it back.

Now we know what Jesus meant when He said I have the power to lay my life down and I have the power to take it up again.

> "Then cometh he to his disciples, and saith unto them, sleep on now and take your rest:"
>
> **Matthew 26:45a**

After Jesus had finished praying the third time, He had won the battle at Gethsemane; He was the Master.

Chapter 9
The Trial

Some of the Jews who saw Lazarus raised from the dead went to the Pharisees and told them what Jesus had done.

"Then gathered the chief priests and Pharisees a council, and said, What do we? for this man doeth many miracles."

"If we let him thus alone, all men will believe on him: and the Romans shall come and take away both our place and nation." [They were worried that their high positions would be gone.]

"And one of them, named Caiaphas, being the high priest that same year, said unto them, Ye know nothing at all,"

"Nor consider that it is expedient for us, that one man should die for the people, and that the whole nation perish not."

"And this spake he not of himself; but being high priest that year, he prophesied that Jesus should die for that nation;" [The word prophesied used here means to speak under inspiration.]

The high priest who offered the yearly sacrifice for the sins of the people had just offered Jesus.

"And not for that nation only, but that also he should gather together in one the children of God that were scattered abroad."

"Then from that day forth they took counsel together for to put him [Jesus] to death."

John 11:47-53

After Jesus was through praying at Gethsemane:

"Judas then, having received a <u>band of men and officers</u> from the chief priests and Pharisees, cometh thither with lanterns and torches and weapons."

"Jesus therefore, knowing all things that should come upon him, went forth, and said unto them, Whom seek ye?"

"They answered him, Jesus of Nazareth. Jesus saith unto them, I am he. And Judas also, which betrayed him, stood with them."

"As soon then as he had said unto them, I am he, <u>they</u> went <u>backward, and fell to the ground.</u>"

This lets us know that even though Jesus had been obedient unto death by placing his life into the Father's hand, the Father hadn't yet offered His Son into the hands of the High Priest. The soldiers couldn't touch him.

"Then asked he them again, Whom seek ye? And they said, Jesus of Nazareth."

"Jesus answered, I have told ye that I am he: <u>if therefore ye seek me, let these go their way:</u>" [Jesus ordered their release.]

"That the saying might be fulfilled, which he spake, Of them which thou gavest me have I lost none."

"Then Simon Peter having a sword drew it and smote the high priest's servant, and cut off his right ear. The servant's name was Mal'chus."

"Then said Jesus unto Peter, Put up thy sword into the sheath: the cup which My Father hath given me, shall I not drink it?"

At this moment, the Father gave his only begotten Son into the hand of Caiaphas the high priest as a sacrifice for the sin of the world; only after the disciples were released.

"Then the band and the captain and officers of the Jews took Jesus and bound him,"

"And led him away to Annas first; for he was father in law to Caiaphas, which was the high priest that same year."

"Now Caiaphas was he, which gave counsel to the Jews, that it was expedient that one man should die for the people."

John 18:3-14

Caiaphas sent Jesus to Pilate, the governor, a Roman procurator of Judea. Caiaphas wanted Pilate to have Jesus crucified.

"For he [Pilate] knew that for envy they [the chief priests] had delivered him." [Jesus]

"When he [Pilate] was set down on the judgment seat his wife sent unto him, saying, Have thou nothing to do with that just man: for I have suffered many things this day in a dream because of him."

"But the chief priests and elders persuaded the multitude that they should ask Barabbas, and destroy Jesus."

Matthew 27:18-20

"And the governor said, Why, what evil hath he done? But they cried out more, saying, Let him be crucified."

"When Pilate saw that he could prevail nothing, but that rather a tumult was made, he took water, and washed his hands before the multitude, saying, I am innocent of the blood of <u>this</u> <u>just</u> <u>person</u>: see ye to it."

"Then answered all the people, and said, <u>His</u> <u>blood</u> <u>be</u> <u>on</u> <u>us,</u> <u>and</u> <u>on</u> <u>our</u> <u>children."</u>

"Then released he Barabbas unto them: and when he had scourged Jesus, he delivered him to be crucified."

Matthew 27:23-26

This has to be the tragedy of the ages. The one who had cut the covenant with Abraham was on trial before the very High Priesthood that He had established.

He came to make good the promises of the covenant. He came to make them sons and daughters. He came to establish a New Covenant with his own blood.

They crucified Him.

Chapter 10
The Cross

"Then the soldiers of the governor took Jesus into the common hall, and gathered unto him the whole band of soldiers."

And they stripped him, and put on him a scarlet robe."

"And when they had platted a crown of thorns, they put it upon his head, and a reed in his right hand: and they bowed the knee before him, and mocked him, saying, Hail King of the Jews!"

"And they spit upon him, and took the reed, and smote him on the head."

"And after that they had mocked him, they took the robe off from him, and put his own raiment on him, and led him away to crucify him."

"And as they came out, they found a man of Cyrene, Simon by name: him they compelled to bear his cross."

"And when they were come unto a place called Golgotha, this is to say, a place of a skull,

"They gave him vinegar to drink mingled with gall: and when he had tasted thereof, he would not drink."

"And they crucified him, [nailing him to the cross] and parted his garments, casting lots: that it might be fulfilled which was spoken by the prophet, THEY PARTED MY GARMENTS AMONG THEM, AND UPON MY VESTURE DID THEY CAST LOTS."

"And sitting down they watched him there;"

"And set up over his head his accusation written, THIS IS JESUS THE KING OF THE JEWS."

"Then were there two thieves crucified with him, one on the right hand, and another on the left."

"And they that passed by reviled him, wagging their heads,"

"And saying, Thou that destroyest the temple, and buildest it in three days, save thyself. If thou be the Son of God, come down from the cross."

"Likewise also the chief priests mocking him, with the scribes and elders said,"

"He saved others; himself he cannot save. If he be the King of Israel, let him now come down from the cross, and we will believe him."

"He trusted in God; let him deliver him now, if he will have him: for he said, I am the Son of God."

"The thieves also, which were crucified with him, cast the same in his teeth."

"Now from the <u>sixth</u> hour there was darkness over all the land unto the ninth hour."

Jesus had **died spiritually** at this time. In Second Corinthians 5:21 it says that God made Jesus to be sin. He was separated from God at this time.

"And about the ninth hour Jesus cried with a loud voice, saying, Eli, Eli, lama sabachthani? that is to say, MY GOD, MY GOD, WHY HAST THOU FORSAKEN ME?"

Matthew 27:27-46

50 "Jesus, when he had cried again with a loud voice, yielded up the ghost."

Jesus died **physically** at this time.

"And, behold, the veil of the temple was rent in twain from the top to the bottom; and the earth did quake, and the rocks rent;"

"And the graves were opened; and many bodies of the saints which slept arose,"

"And came out of the graves <u>after</u> his resurrection, and went into the holy city, and appeared unto many."

"Now when the centurion, and they that were with him, watching Jesus, saw the earthquake, and those things that were done, they feared greatly, saying, Truly this was the Son of God."

Matthew 27:50-54

Let's go back to Matthew 27:50, "Jesus, when he had cried again with a load voice, yielded up the ghost." (Physical death had occurred.)

"Then came the soldiers, and brake the legs of the first, and of the other which was crucified with him."

"But when they came to Jesus, and saw that he was dead already, they brake not his legs:"

"But one of the soldiers with a spear pierced his side, and forthwith came there out blood and water."

John 19:32-34

Remember the prayer Jesus prayed in Hebrews 5:7 that loosed the Holy Spirit to raise him from the dead. The instant Jesus died, Satan and his evil spirits were surely there to cast his spirit into hell.

"For Christ also hath once suffered for sins, the just for the unjust, that he might bring us to God, being put to death in the flesh, but <u>quickened</u> [made alive] by the Spirit:"

"By which also he went and preached unto the spirits in prison."

1 Peter 3:18,19

We can see that something else happened when Jesus gave up the ghost. Remember Matthew 27:50,51,

"Jesus, when he had cried again with a loud voice, yielded up the ghost."

"And behold, the veil of the temple was rent in twain [torn in two] **from the top to the bottom; and the earth did quake, and the rocks rent;"**

The Holy Spirit had left the temple and like a bolt of lightening, shot straight to the cross and answered the prayer Jesus had prayed while he was still alive at Gethsemane. The Holy Spirit quickened Jesus, (made him alive.) Jesus immediately over powered Satan and the demon spirits that wanted to cast him into hell.

"Blotting out the handwriting of ordinances that was against us, which was contrary to us, and took it out of the way, nailing it to his cross;"

"And having <u>spoiled</u> [disarmed] **principalities and powers, he made a <u>shew</u>** [spectacle] **of them openly, triumphing over them in it."**
                                        Colossians 2:14,15

Then by the power of the Spirit Jesus went to the spirits in prison and preached to them. He went into the depths of hell and conquered them. Read again 1 Peter 3:18,19.

"I am he that liveth, and was dead; and behold, I am alive for evermore, amen; and have the <u>keys</u> [authority] **of hell and of death."**
                                        Revelations 1:18

The rending of the veil was the rending of the Abrahamic covenant. Annas and Caiaphas had slain the Lamb of God, their last sacrifice before Jehovah. They will slay animals before men, but it will not be accepted by God.

In closing, we should read Psalm 22 which gives a graphic picture of the crucifixion of Jesus. It is more comprehensive than that of Matthew, Mark, or John. This crucifixion scene was written 1000 years before Jesus Christ hung there on the cross, and 600 years before anyone had been crucified.

"My God, My God, why hast thou forsaken me? why art thou so far from helping me, and from the words of my roaring?"

"O my God, I cry in the day time, but thou hearest not; and in the night season, and am not silent."

"But thou art holy, O thou that inhabitest the praises of Israel."

"Our fathers trusted in thee: they trusted, and thou didst deliver them."

"They cried unto thee, and were delivered: they trusted in thee, and were not confounded."

"But I am a worm, and no man; a reproach of men, and despised of the people."

"All they that see me laugh me to scorn: they shoot out the lip, they shake the head, saying,"

"He trusted on the Lord that he would delivery him: Let him deliver him, seeing he delighted in him."

"But thou art he that took me out of the womb: thou didst made me hope when I was upon my mother's breasts."

"I was cast upon thee from the womb: thou art my God from my mother's belly."

"Be not far from me; for trouble is near; for there is none to help."

"Many bulls have compassed me: strong bulls of Bashan have beset me round."

"They gaped upon me with their mouths, as a ravening and a roaring lion."

"I am poured out like water, and all my bones are out of joint: my heart is like wax; it is melted in the midst of my bowels."

"My strength is dried up like a potsherd; and my tongue cleaveth to my jaws; and thou has brought me into the dust of death."

"For dogs have compassed me: the assembly of the wicked have enclosed me: they pierced my hands and my feet."

"I may tell all my bones: they look and stare upon me."

"They part my garments among them, and cast lots upon my vesture."

"But be not thou far from me, O Lord: O my strength, haste thee to help me."

"Deliver my soul from the sword; my darling from the power of the dog."

"Save me from the Lion's mouth: <u>for</u> <u>thou</u> <u>hast</u> <u>heard</u> <u>me</u> from the horns of the unicorns."

Psalm 22:1-21

Chapter 11

The Lord's Supper in the Light of All Four Gospels

Jesus **Institutes** the Lord's Supper and the New Covenant.

W hy four gospels? When the Father God inspired four men to write the gospels, it was to be **their** account of what they saw and/or what they heard about the life of Jesus.

A **reason** for the writing of four gospels is that one gospel would not have been sufficient to present the many sides of Christ's person. Each of the writers views Him from a different aspect. Matthew presents Him as King, Mark as Conqueror (and servant), Luke as son of man, and John as Son of God. The viewing of Christ is like the viewing of a huge building — only one side can be taken in at one time.

"And many other signs truly did Jesus in the presence of his disciples, which are not written in this book:"

"But these are written, that ye might believe that Jesus is the Christ, the Son of God; and that believing ye might have life through his name."

John 20:30,31

41

After studying all four gospels, it becomes evident that Luke gave the most comprehensive report, dealing with relevant details concerning the Lord's Supper.

"And he [Jesus] said unto them, With desire I have desired to eat this passover with you before I suffer:"

"For I say unto you, I will not any more eat thereof, until it be fulfilled in the kingdom of God."

"And he took the cup, and gave thanks, and said, Take this, and <u>divide</u> it among yourselves:"

"For I say unto you, I will not drink of the fruit of the vine, until the kingdom of God shall come."

"And he took bread, and gave thanks, and brake it, and gave unto them, saying, This is my body which is given for you: this do in remembrance of Me."

"Likewise also the cup <u>after</u> <u>supper</u>, [no bread] saying, This cup is the new testament [Covenant] in my blood, which is shed for you."

Luke 22:15-20

Let's also look at Luke 22:20 in the Living Bible.

"<u>After</u> <u>supper</u> he [Jesus] gave them <u>another</u> glass of wine, [no bread] saying, This wine is the token of God's <u>new</u> agreement [covenant] to save you — an agreement [covenant] <u>sealed</u> <u>with</u> <u>the</u> <u>blood</u> <u>I</u> <u>shall</u> <u>pour</u> <u>out</u> to purchase back your souls."

Luke 22:20 (TLB)

After gathering all the relevant facts from the gospels concerning the Lord's Supper, and how we should partake, this is what I believe the Holy Spirit has shown me.

First you take the cup and **divide** it among yourselves. Each person has a cup and takes a portion of the fruit of the vine (wine) which represents Jesus' blood that was shed at **Calvary**.

Next, take a piece of bread broken from a loaf. (They didn't have sliced bread at that time, so now it would be fine to break a piece from a slice of bread.) Then dip the piece of bread into the wine and it becomes what the scriptures call a **sop**. This sop represents the blood that was shed for us at Calvary, and His body that was given for us. This we are to do often in remembrance of Christ.

After the Lord's Supper, you take **another cup** of wine, without any bread. This represents the blood Jesus shed at Gethsemane while he was offering His life into the Father's hands, before the sins of the world were laid on Him. This blood seals the covenant God made with Abraham and his seed which is **Christ**. This blood had to be shed before Jesus was made sin for us.

> **"And he [Jesus] was withdrawn from them about a stone's cast, and kneeled down, and prayed."**
>
> **"Saying, Father, if thou be willing, remove this cup from me: nevertheless not my will, but thine, be done:"**
>
> **"And there appeared an angel unto him from heaven, strengthening him."**
>
> **"And being in an agony he prayed more earnestly: and his sweat was as it were great drops of blood falling down to the ground."**
>
> **Luke 22:41-44**

This blood **sealed** the Abrahamic Covenant when Christ sprinkled it on the real mercy seat in the heavenly Holy of Holies. This blood had to come from the holy Lamb of God that had not had the sins of the world laid on Him.

> **"...Christ came with God's new and better way."** [covenant]
>
> **"He came as High Priest of this better system** [new covenant] **which we now have. He went into that greater, perfect tabernacle in heaven, not made by men**

43

nor part of this world, and once for all took blood into that inner room, the Holy of Holies, and sprinkled it on the mercy seat; but it was not the blood of goats and calves. No, he took his own blood, and with it he, by himself, made sure of our eternal salvation."

Hebrews 9:10-12 (TLB)

Let's again go over a few scriptures so they are fresh in our hearts.

"Now to Abraham and his <u>seed</u> were the promises made. He saith not, and to seeds, as of many; but as of one, And to thy <u>seed</u>, which is Christ."

Galatians 3:16

"But now in Christ Jesus ye who sometimes were far off [without a covenant] are made nigh by the blood of Christ."

"For he is our peace, who hath made <u>both</u> <u>one</u>, [Jews and Gentiles] and hath broken down the middle wall of partition between us;"

"Having abolished in his flesh the enmity, even the law of commandments contained in ordinances; for to <u>make</u> [create] in himself of <u>twain</u> [two] <u>one</u> <u>new</u> <u>man</u>, so making peace;"

"And that he might reconcile both unto God <u>in</u> <u>one</u> <u>body</u> by the cross, having slain the enmity thereby:"

Ephesians 2:13-16

Remember, through Abraham came **the body, the Word entered the body. The two (twain) became one.** This one was Christ. **Christ was Abraham's seed.**

"And if ye be Christ's, <u>then</u> <u>are</u> <u>ye</u> <u>Abraham's</u> <u>seed,</u> <u>and</u> <u>heirs</u> <u>according</u> <u>to</u> <u>the</u> <u>promise.</u>"

Galatians 3:29

After the seed of Abraham (Christ) sprinkled his blood on the Mercy Seat, he had fulfilled the Abrahamic Covenant. Then, and only then, did we become heirs to the redemptive work of Christ at Calvary.

When the Father God offered His only begotten son for our salvation and our healing, Jesus Christ was beaten, torn and bruised, and pierced for the healing of our bodies. The scriptures say the sins of the world were laid on Him, and he became sin for us. On the cross He dies for us spiritually and then physically by the shedding of His blood.

Why did this happen?

"For God so loved the world that he gave his only begotten son, that whosoever believeth in him should not perish but have everlasting life."

"For God sent not his son into the world to condemn the world; but that the world through him <u>might</u> be saved.

"He that believeth on him is not condemned: but he that believeth not is condemned already, because he hath not believed in the name of the only begotten Son of God."

John 3:16-18

"For by grace are ye saved through faith; and that not of yourselves: it is the gift of God:"

"Not of works, lest any man should boast."

Ephesians 2:8,9

"That if thou shalt <u>confess</u> [say] with thy mouth the Lord Jesus, and believe in thine heart that God has raised him from the dead, thou shalt be saved."

"For with the heart man believeth unto righteousness; and with the mouth confession is made unto salvation."

Romans 10:9,10

Here is a simple prayer for those who would like to be born again.

Jesus, I believe you died for my sins, and God has raised you from the dead. Come into my heart, and be my Lord. Amen.

Notes Concerning the Lord's Supper

Scriptures concerning the Lord's Supper are found in Matthew, Mark, Luke, and John.

Matthew 26:23 and Mark 14:20 tells us they dipped the bread.

Luke 22:17 — Jesus had them **divide** the cup (wine).

Luke 22:19 — Jesus gave them bread. Because of what Matthew and Mark wrote, we know they dipped the bread. No bread was eaten that wasn't dipped.

John 13:26 teaches when the bread was dipped into the wine it was called a sop. The sop represented the Body of Christ, bruised and beaten, with the blood pouring out unto death. This blood was shed at **Calvary** for our sins.

Luke gives us the most detailed account of the Lord's Supper. Luke 22:20 states that Jesus gave them another cup after the Lord's Supper was over. This cup was served with no bread. Jesus said, "This cup is the New Covenant in My blood which is shed for you." Jesus wasn't carrying the sins of the world when he shed this blood. This blood was the blood of a perfect man without sin. This blood was shed at Gethsemane when Jesus was offering his life to the Father through prayer.

The Father God accepted the prayer of Jesus as He was offering His life for our sins. This completed the covenant God had made with Abraham and Abraham's seed, which is Christ. The Father supernaturally drew the pure, sin free blood through the pores of His Son to prove the Abrahamic covenant had been cut. This blood from a perfect man would be sprinkled on the mercy seat in the heavenly Holy of Holies. This blood would complete and seal the Covenant God made with Abraham.

With this information fresh in our hearts, we can go back to the other scriptures concerning the Lord's Supper and see what Luke wrote shines a light on the other gospels and they all must harmonize. What happened in one gospel had to happen in all four gospels.

To contact the author:
Email:
atreeoflife@cox.net

PivotPointPublishing.com

What Really Happened In the Garden of Eden

This teaching is so different from traditional teachings about the Garden of Eden and what took place there, but it will in no way go against sound Bible doctrine. In fact, it will strengthen it.

As you enter the Garden of Eden, you will see many things that have been hidden in the Scriptures as the Holy Spirit unveils them for us. You will either be thrilled or alarmed at the discoveries that unfold as you read through this book.